THE SPIRIT OF CHRISMATION

By: Daniel Michalski

SAINT SHENOUDA PRESS

THE SPIRIT OF CHRISMATION

By: Daniel Michalski

ST SHENOUDA PRESS
SYDNEY, AUSTRALIA
2023

THE SPIRIT OF CHRISMATION

By: Daniel Michalski

COPYRIGHT © 2023
St. Shenouda Press

ST SHENOUDA PRESS
8419 Putty Rd,
Putty, NSW, 2330
Sydney, Australia

www.stshenoudapress.com

ISBN 13: 978-0-6457703-4-6

CONTENTS

Acknowlegment

To all those who seek the truth in Christ our God, especially those who are inquirers or catechumens in the Holy Orthodox Church of God

Special thanks to Abouna Michael Maximous of St. Basil American Coptic Orthodox Church and Abouna Mark Paul of St. Paul's Coptic Abbey for reviewing and suggestions during the production of this work

What is Chrismation?

Chrismation is the Sacrament [1] of anointing with Myron[2] oil and laying on of hands by a priest with apostolic succession. It is also called Myron, Confirmation[3] , or Unction[4] . It is a Sacrament ordained by Christ and is a vital part of our salvation. Chrismation directly follows Baptism.

The Baptized person is anointed by the priest or Bishop[5], the priest or Bishop prays over the recipient, lays his

---

1 A Sacrament in Orthodoxy is physical matter used by God to convey grace. It is sometimes said to have an outward sign (matter) pointing to and conveying a spiritual grace.

2 Myron, also called Chrism or anointing oil, is a holy oil compound used by the Church to consecrate (set apart as holy) the Baptismal waters, consecrate the Altar, and to perform the Sacrament of Chrismation by anointing the body of the person being Chrismated. It is made from two oils and various spices. It is a separate compound from the Oil of Catechumens (used to make someone a Catechumen through anointing) and the Oil of Unction (used to anoint the sick). Myron is made by the highest Bishop in any of the Oriental Orthodox Churches.

3 It is called this in the Western Churches primarily

4 Unction is a treatment, healing, or consecration with the use of oil.

5 A Bishop is the Chief or High Priest of a region, having multiple Churches and priests under him in authority.

hands on them, and breathes on them to receive the Holy Spirit. In the early Church, the deaconess[6] would assist[7] by Chrismating the adult women at the permission of the Bishop to preserve modesty. Now, the priest or Bishop does the Chrismation of women, but only on the parts of the body which are appropriate for him to touch.

The priest or Bishop, when He prays over the recipient, is praying that the Baptized may receive the Spirit and be a vessel for Him, consecrated for eternal life. In the Coptic Rite [8] the prayers include: "Grant the Holy Spirit in the pouring out of the Holy Myron. Let it be a life-giving seal and a confirmation to your servants, through your only-begotten Son, Jesus Christ, our Lord," and, "In His name receive the Holy Spirit and be a purified vessel." Similarly, in the Armenian Rite, the priest or Bishop says among other prayers: "This sweet oil, which is poured out upon your forehead in the name of Jesus Christ, be a seal of incorruptible[9] heavenly gifts," and, "May this divine seal direct your journey towards eternal life so that you may not be shaken."

---

6 Deaconess is a female Deacon, assistant to the priest, who in the Early Church assisted with Baptizing women

7 Apostolic Constitutions III.XV, III.XVI VIII.XXVIII. Long quotes given below

8 The Orthodox Church has several Rites or orders for worship, prayer, and Sacraments: Coptic, Syriac, Armenian, Ge'ez, and Indian. The Coptic Rite is used by the Coptic or Egyptian Church, the Syriac by the Syriac (Syrian) Church, the Armenian by the Armenian Church, the Ge'ez by the Ethiopian and Eritrean Churches, and the Indian (heavily influenced by the Syriac Rite) by the Indian Church. These all have the same faith, simply with different styles, tunes, and historical developments.

9 Incorruptible=unable to perish or become corrupted. God's gifts are unable to perish as He is beyond any corruption or decay.

Although it is not directly described in the Scriptures as ordained by Christ, we know from the Holy Tradition[10] of the Church that this Sacrament was given to the Apostles (and thence to the Bishops who succeeded them) for the receiving of the Holy Spirit. Chrismation is foreshadowed in the Old Testament, mentioned in passing in the New Testament, described and explained by the Fathers, and practiced as part of the Baptismal Rite in the One Holy Catholic and Apostolic Orthodox Church[11] .

When exactly Christ instituted the Sacrament of Chrismation is unclear. Some fathers have said at the Last Supper, others during the ten days between the Ascension[12] and Pentecost[13] . But all agree Christ gave the laying on of hands to receive the Holy Spirit to the Apostles. Many fathers [14] say explicitly or implicitly

---

10 Holy Tradition or the Apostolic Tradition/Tradition of the Apostles in Orthodoxy has two parts: the Bible or Scriptures, which are the written account by guidance of the Holy Spirit of God's revelation; and the Oral Tradition, which is the sacred teachings passed down by the Apostles through the Bishops who have preserved the orthodox (right teaching) faith. The Tradition, in written and oral form is all one unit of the faith of the Apostles for the Church.

11 The One Holy Catholic Apostolic and Orthodox Church is the formal name for what is called the Oriental Orthodox Church. This name means the Church is unified, sanctified or made holy by the Spirit of God, universal or encompassing and welcoming all people of the world, has its foundation in Christ's Apostles, and is orthodox-maintaining proper faith and practice.

12 Ascension is the feast day commemorating the ascension of Christ into heaven forty days after His Resurrection from the dead, and Pentecost is the feast day commemorating the descent of the Holy Spirit on the Apostles which took place ten days later. Both are celebrated yearly and their dates are based on the date of Easter for that year.

13 Dionysius Bar Salibi, Trans. Baby Varghese, Commentaries on Myron and Baptism (Piscatawy, NJ: Gorgias Press, 2012), 16.

14 E.g., St. Athanasius, St. Cyril of Jerusalem, St. Basil, St. Clement of Alexandria, St. Dionysius

that Christ also directly gave the Apostles the tradition of anointing with oil, even giving them the first Myron, directly. Some fathers [15] say that the Apostles instituted the use of oil which they had blessed when they could no longer lay hands on everyone, and gave this right to the Bishops who succeeded them. While some of the history of the Sacrament may thus be unclear, and we should allow for diversity of opinions on this point, the core of the Sacramental origin remains the same. Namely, the Sacrament of giving the Holy Spirit through the laying on of hands and anointing with Myron oil is from the Apostles under the direction of Christ and is therefore of Apostolic and Divine authority.

Chrismation, as a Sacrament, involves the use by God of matter as an instrument of salvation[16]. Matter is transformed and worked through not just to signify or indicate a spiritual reality, but to make that reality present. Michael Papazian, summarizing St. Pseudo-Dionysius the Areopagite[17] writes, "A sacrament in the broadest sense is God's use of a material thing, something that may have little value but from which divine graces flow and through which we encounter God."[18]

Bar Salibi, St. Moses Bar Kepha, St. Jacob of Serugh, St. Jacob of Edessa, St. Pseudo-Dionysius, and St. Fabianus.

15 E.g., HH Pope Shenouda III, Anba Mettaous el-Sourian, and HG Bishop Youssef.

16 Salvation is the process of our being given new natures, cleansed from sin, and renewed in the likeness of God, becoming "participants of the divine nature" (2 Peter 1:4).

17 The author who wrote under the name Dionysius the Areopagite was probably a 5th-6th century Syrian monk holding to Miaphysite Christology; possibly St. Peter the Fuller.

18 Michael Papazian, The Doctor of Mercy (Collegeville, MN:Liturgical Press Academic, 2019), 158.

In the Holy Eucharist, the bread and wine truly become the Body and Blood of Christ. In Baptism the water is sanctified and changes in essence from ordinary water to holy, purifying water. As in these Sacraments, in Chrismation the Myron oil is changed from natural oil to holy, sanctified oil. The oil, infused with Fire of the Spirit conveys to the recipient the purification of sins and the permanent indwelling of the Holy Spirit.

The oil, or Myron, with which the Baptized person is anointed, is the same oil used to bless the various functions of the Church. The Church building, the Altar, the Baptismal water, the priests when they are ordained- all these are anointed with the sacred Myron oil to consecrate them.

The Sacrament of Chrismation imparts to the Baptized person the name of Christian- anointed one. By Chrismation we are given both a right to the name Christian and the spiritual power to fight the spiritual fight, striving towards the end of perfection in union with Christ our God. Chrismation acts as armor for Christians, giving them protection and spiritual weaponry to fight the devil and be protected against his attacks. This spiritual weaponry is the gifts of the Spirit common to all Christians-wisdom, understanding, counsel, fortitude, knowledge, piety, and fear of the Lord.

In Chrismation we are indwelt with the Holy Spirit. He dwelt in Adam by nature, but when Adam fell from eternal life by his own will and was exiled from the Paradise of Joy, he lost the indwelling Spirit. The Spirit would come temporarily on certain members of the old covenants[19]

19 A covenant is an oath-bound promise sealed in blood, and it is by this means that God has made Himself known to humanity throughout history. The older Covenants (with Adam,

. In the New Covenant[20], the Holy Spirit is given to all God's people as a permanent possession. The Holy Spirit, entering us at Chrismation, plants within us the seeds that may become with our cooperation the fruits of the Spirit- love, joy, peace, patience, kindness, generosity, faithfulness, gentleness, self-control (Galatians 5:22-23).

Chrismation seals the New Covenant to the believer. When the sign of the Cross, through which our Lord abolished death and brought life and resurrection to light, is made on our bodies, we are sealed as members of the New Covenant. Thereby, we are made welcome guests at His Table; that is, we may eat freely of the Holy Eucharist[21] - the New Covenant sacrifice meal. By this sealing as New Covenant members, we are sealed, marked out, for the day of resurrection. Chrismation is a sort of stamp, sealing us as belonging to Christ, marking our bodies as members of Christ so that when He comes to judge the living and the dead we may be raised up as His own.

All these are by the Spirit through the priests of Christ with apostolic succession[22]. Our Lord, God, and Savior Jesus Christ gave His Apostles authority to forgive sins: "When he had said this, he breathed on them and said to

---

Noah, Abraham, Moses, and David) pointed to and prepared for Christ. We become living members of the New Covenant through Baptism.

20 The final, eternal Covenant established by Christ which promises forgiveness of sins and immortality through His Body and Blood.

21 Eucharist, also called Communion or the Lord's Supper, means thanksgiving. It is the Sacrament whereby we partake of the true Body and Blood of Christ for remission of sins and receive the seed of our resurrected, glofirified bodies.

22 Apostolic succession means the chain or succession of ordination of priests and Bishops going back to the Apostles.

them, 'Receive the Holy Spirit. If you forgive the sins of any, they are forgiven them; if you retain the sins of any, they are retained.'"(John 20:22-23) This power to forgive sins is not something magical or by the priest's nature, but through, by, and in the Holy Spirit.

It is this Person of the Spirit which is given to us in the Sacrament of Chrismation by the laying on of the hands of the priesthood. As it is only the Apostles and their successors who possess this special spiritual authority, so only those who have proper apostolic succession may Chrismate and we must be anointed with the oil of Chrismation by a true priest- one who has apostolic succession -in order to benefit from this holy and necessary Sacrament.

Chrismation is necessary for salvation. It is not optional; it is not an afterthought. Chrismation completes and perfects Baptism which Sacrament is not finished without the Anointing of the Myron. This may be seen by the fact that the Baptismal water itself is consecrated with the Myron.

Stemming from its completing the act of Baptism, Chrismation (again) is what armors the Christian for life. It is the Holy Spirit within the Christian who works every day through the Sacraments, through repentance, through prayer, through Liturgy[23], and through conviction of sin. The Spirit given in Chrismation remains and works in the Christian throughout their lives. In that way, the Christian life may be seen as a working out of, or a living in and through, our Chrismation as well as our Baptism.

---

23 Liturgy, from "work of the people" in Greek, is the Divine Service of public worship.

To summarize, in Holy Chrismation we receive the permanent indwelling of the Holy Spirit, the purifying Fire of holiness. In Chrismation we receive Divine wisdom to know the mysteries[24] of God, and are sealed for the day of redemption (the glorious resurrection). Christ ordained Chrismation as a Sacrament that perfects Baptism and gave it to His Apostles who passed on their authority and power to the Priesthood.

---

24 Mystery = a reality beyond intellectual speculation or comprehension.

TIMING OF CHRISMATION

The Sacrament of Chrismation or Myron is given along with the Sacrament of Baptism. From the beginning the receiving of the Spirit was united with but also distinct from Baptism. One should not receive Christ's Covenant and forgiveness of sins without also receiving the Spirit of Christ at the same time. The two Sacraments are bound together. Through the sacred waters of Baptism our sins are remitted and we are justified, among many other blessings. Through the Holy Myron of Chrismation we receive the Holy Spirit. When we have received these saving blessings, we are then able to partake of the Body and Blood of Christ our God in the Sacrament of the Holy Eucharist.

In the early Church, Chrismation in some places was given right before[25] Baptism and in some places it was given right after Baptism. The Church now does the latter. This should not bother us as administering Chrismation in either way keeps it directly connected to Holy Baptism.

---

25 Per class at St. Athanasius and St. Cyril Coptic Orthodox Theological School

St. Cyril of Jerusalem wrote, "In the same manner to you also, after you had come up from the pool of the sacred streams [Baptism], were given the Unction, the emblem of that wherewith Christ was anointed; and this is the Holy Spirit...you were anointed with ointment, having been made partakers and fellows of Christ.[26] "

Armenian Archbishop Malachia Ormanian wrote, "holy anointing is administered conjointly with that Sacrament by the priest who performs the Baptism. [27]"

---

26 Cyril of Jerusalem, Trans. R.W. Church, Lectures on the Christian Sacraments, (Crestwood, NY: SVS Press, 1977), 64-65. Language updated to reflect modern speech.

27 Archbishop Malachia Ormanian, The Church of Armenia (Burbank, CA: WDACNA, 2007), 115.

CHRISMATION IN THE
OLD TESTAMENT

The Old Testament is a tapestry of types and shadows pointing us to the good things of the New Covenant. When read properly, seeing the hidden and spiritual meaning behind the literal words, Christ is everywhere throughout these sacred Scriptures. In types, things which resemble and point us to a deeper reality, it foreshadows Christ. The Sacrament of Chrismation, one of the blessings of the New Covenant Christ brought to us, is foreshadowed in the Old Testament. Oil throughout the Bible is often connected to the Spirit, and the Spirit to oil.

Chrismation is seen in Jacob's anointing the rock[28] after his dream of the ladder that went up to heaven, which the Church teaches is a type of St. Mary, though whom the King of Heaven came into the world. After he awoke from the dream, he anointed the rock he had slept on with oil and called the place Bethel (House of God). Likewise, when we receive Christ and His blessing in Baptism, we

28 Saint Ephrem the Syrian makes this comparison of Jacob anointing the rock to Chrismation in his hymn on Chrismation.

are anointed with the Myron oil by the priest in order to enter the Church- the House of God. We are compared to rocks as Christ told those who trusted in lineage for salvation that He was able to raise up children to Abraham from rocks.

Chrismation is seen in the anointing of the Old Covenant priests. "You shall bring Aaron and his sons to the entrance of the tent of meeting and wash them with water…Then you shall take some of the blood that is on the altar and some of the anointing oil and sprinkle it on Aaron and his vestments and on his sons and his sons' vestments with him;" (Ex. 29:4, 21).

After washing, they were anointed, typifying the cleansing waters of Baptism and the grace of the Spirit in Chrismation. In Baptism we are washed with pure water and sprinkled with the Blood of Christ which cleanses us from all sin. Likewise, all who are Baptized and Chrismated become part of the general, royal priesthood of believers. (This, of course, is to be distinguished from the particular Melchizedek priesthood of those who receive the Sacrament of Priesthood and are thus alone able to offer the Eucharist and grant absolution).

Chrismation is seen in the story of Judith. "She removed the sackcloth she had been wearing, took off her widow's garments, bathed her body with water, and anointed herself with precious ointment. She combed her hair, put on a tiara, and dressed herself in the festive attire that she used to wear while her husband Manasseh was living." (Judith 10:13) Just as Judith washed herself with water and anointed herself before going forth with a crown to fight the wicked king, so the Christian is Baptized and Chrismated and then brought to the Altar wearing a red ribbon and goes forth with that spiritual power to fight the devil.

Chrismation is seen in God's depiction of saving His Old Covenant Church through the prophet Ezekiel. In speaking of His redemption of Israel, the Lord said, "Then I bathed you with water and washed off the blood from you and anointed you with oil." (Ezek. 16:9) Again, there is a connection between the purity received in washing from uncleanness and being anointed with oil.

In addition to types, Chrismation is seen in the promise of the Spirit being poured upon the Incarnate Logos [29]. "The Spirit of the Lord God is upon me, because the Lord has anointed me" (Is. 61:1). A connection is made here between receiving the Spirit and being anointed. Just as Christ was anointed with the Spirit, so Christians are anointed with the Spirit at Chrismation. Indeed, the idea of being anointed with oil exists in the very name Christian, one is christened. This christening or Chrismation Isaiah foretold of Christ, and those who are united with Christ through Baptism (Rom. 6:4-5) share with Him in this anointing from the Holy One (1 John 2:20).

---

29 Logos is the Greek for Word.

CHRISMATION IN THE NEW TESTAMENT

The New Testament appears to contain no direct reference to Chrismation or its establishment by Christ. However, through the oral Apostolic Tradition of the Church, which St. Paul says we should regard as equal to and just as binding as the Scriptures (2 Thess. 2:15), we are told that Christ our God gave Chrismation or receiving the Spirit by the laying on of hands to the Apostles.

The Church tells us by the Spirit, exemplified by the quotes from the early church fathers noted below, that the Apostles passed on this sacred Myron oil to the Bishops who succeeded them in the priesthood[30] . Some of this Myron has from their time been mixed into each successive batch of Myron, meaning the oil which the Church uses to Chrismate the Baptized even today contains part of and is essentially linked to the oil the Apostles used to Chrismate.

---

30 Some modern Bishops hold that the Apostles did not themselves use Myron in Chrismation but only laying on of hands, others hold the Apostles themselves used the Myron oil.

There are a number of passages in the New Testament which receive greater clarity and context through understanding this Apostolic Tradition. St. Peter told the multitudes at Pentecost both to be Baptized for the remission of sins and then receive the Holy Spirit: "Peter said to them, 'Repent, and be baptized every one of you in the name of Jesus Christ so that your sins may be forgiven; and you will receive the gift of the Holy Spirit.'" (Acts 2:38) This is explained later in Acts where it was said to be through the laying on of the Apostles' hands that the Holy Spirit was given: "Now when the apostles at Jerusalem heard that Samaria had accepted the word of God, they sent Peter and John to them. The two went down and prayed for them that they might receive the Holy Spirit, for as yet the Spirit had not come upon any of them; they had only been baptized in the name of the Lord Jesus. Then Peter and John laid their hands on them, and they received the Holy Spirit." (Acts 8:14-17)

Throughout Acts there is a separation between being Baptized and receiving the Spirit even whilst they are tied together; and there is a tying of receiving the indwelling of the Holy Spirit to the laying on of the Apostles' hands. The one exception to this general rule, when the Gentiles received the Holy Spirit and then were Baptized by St. Peter (Acts 10:34-48), elicited surprise by the Jewish Christians who were present and was an extraordinary gift of God to demonstrate that He was saving all the nations.

Understanding Chrismation means we can see that along with being Baptized for the remission of sins, the Apostles Chrismated them- laid their hands on the Baptized and anointed them with the Myron. Through this anointing and laying on of hands, the Baptized person received the Holy Spirit. To this day, the priests and Bishops with apostolic succession, following the Tradition of the fathers, keep this practice. They anoint and lay their hand on the person they are Chrismating for the reception of the Holy Spirit.

Saint Paul also indicates that it is through laying on of the hands of the Priesthood that gift of the Spirit is given: "Do not disregard the gift which is in you, which was given to you through prophecy, by the laying on of the hands of the priesthood [31]." (1 Tim. 4:14, translation my own) This gift is the Spirit which was given to St. Timothy through the laying on of hands by a priest or priests. Saint Timothy is thus reminded that unlike the false teachers who will come (4:1), he has been given the Spirit and should not rely on human strength to do the work of the ministry but rely on the Holy Spirit within him [32].

It is by the Anointing we have from the Holy One that we know all things: "But you have been Anointed by the Holy One, and all of you have knowledge...As for you, the Anointing that you received from him abides in you, and so you do not need anyone to teach you. But as his Anointing teaches you about all things, and is true and is not a lie, and just as it has taught you, abide in him." (1 John 2:20, 27) Christians are said by St. John to have been anointed with an Anointing that is living within us, teaching us, giving us wisdom and knowledge. This is not a force or an attribute but a Person, even the Holy Spirit Whom Christ promised to give the disciples so that they

---

31 While this word is often translated in English as elders or presbytery, the word is the same as the term for priest and there is a theological aversion to a Christian priesthood behind the common English translations.

32 This passage may also refer to the giving of the gift of Priesthood

might be taught all the truth by Him (16:13). The Spirit is said to be an Anointing as we received Him through Chrismation, through anointing with the Myron. Again, we did not receive the Spirit apart from Chrismation nor did we receive the Myron oil only without the Spirit. The Spirit and Fire are in the the Myron and we receive that Anointing, the Holy Spirit, in our hearts when we are anointed with the Myron.

CHRISMATION IN WORDS OF THE EARLY CHURCH FATHERS

"God of Hosts (lit. powers), the helper of every soul that turns to You and that comes under the mighty hand of Your only-begotten, we invoke You to work in this chrism a divine and heavenly energy through the divine and unseen powers of our Lord and Saviour Jesus Christ, in order that they who have been baptized, and who are of being the anointed sign of with the it with saving the impress cross of the onlybegotten, by which cross Satan and every opposing power was routed and triumphed over, they also, as being regenerated and renewed through the washing of regeneration (Titus iii. 5), may become partakers of the gift of the holy Spirit, and being made secure by this seal (i Cor. xv. 53), may continue steadfast and unmoveable, unhurt and inviolate, free from harsh treatment and intrigue, in the franchise of the faith and full knowledge of the truth, awaiting to the end the heavenly hopes of life and eternal promises of our Lord and Saviour Jesus Christ, through whom to You (is) the glory and the strength both now and to all the ages of the ages. Amen.[33] " (St. Serapion, Bishop of Thmuis, 4th century)

"For on that day the Lord Jesus, after supping with His disciples, and washing their feet, according to the tradition which our predecessors received from the holy apostles and left to us, taught them to prepare the chrism. That washing of their feet signifies our baptism, as it is completed and confirmed by the unction of the holy chrism. [34]" (St. Fabianus, [Pope Fabian of Rome])

"Anointed also must he of necessity be, who is baptized, that having received the chrism—that is, unction, he may be the anointed of God, and have within him the grace of Christ. [35]" (Council of Carthage, 257 AD)

"We call all believers Christians on account of the mystical Chrism[36] " (St. Augustine)

"The flesh, indeed, is washed, in order that the soul may be cleansed; the flesh is anointed, that the soul may be consecrated; the flesh is signed (with the cross), that the soul too may be fortified; the flesh is shadowed with the imposition of hands, that the soul also maybe illuminated[37] " (Scholar Tertullian)

---

33 Serapion of Thmuis, Trans. Dr. G. Wobbermin,Bishop Sarapion's Prayer Book (London: SPCK, 1899), 76. Language updated to reflect modern speech.

34 Philip Schaff, ed., The Complete Ante-Nicene & Nicene and Post-Nicene Church Fathers Collection, Vol. 8, Epistles of Fabian, II.1, by Fabian of Rome (London: Catholic Way, 2014).

35 Ibid., Vol. 14, The Synod held at Carthage by Augustine of Hippo (London: Catholic Way, 2014).

36 Ibid., Vol. 9, The City of God, by Augustine of Hippo (London: Catholic Way, 2014).

37 Ibid., Vol. 3, On the Resurrection of the Flesh, Ch. 8, by Tertullian (London: Catholic Way, 2014).

"Wherefore we are called Christians on this account, because we are anointed with the oil of God. [38]" (St. Theophilus of Antioch)

"Being therefore made partakers of Christ,[you are properly called Christs, and of you God said, Touch not My Christs, or anointed. Now you were made Christs by receiving the emblem of the Holy Spirit; and all things were in a figure wrought in you, because you are figures of Christ...you also, after you had come up from the pool of the sacred streams, were given the Unction, the emblem of that wherewith Christ was anointed; and this is the Holy Spirit...But beware of supposing this to be plain ointment. For as the Bread of the Eucharist, after the invocation of the Holy Spirit, is mere bread no longer, but the Body of Christ, so also this holy ointment is no longer simple ointment, but the gift of Christ; and by the presence of His Godhead, it causes in us the Holy Spirit. It is symbolically applied to your forehead and your other senses; and while your body is anointed with visible ointment, your soul is sanctified by the Holy and life-giving Spirit. [39]" (St. Cyril of Jerusalem)

"There you did dip [i.e., were Baptized], you came to the priest. What did he say to you? 'God the Father Almighty, 'he says, 'who has regenerated you by water and the Holy Spirit, and has forgiven you your sins, himself anoint you unto eternal life.' See whereunto you are anointed; 'unto eternal life,' he says. Do not set this life before that life... Do not choose that wherein you were not anointed, but choose that wherein you were anointed, so as to prefer

---

38 Ibid., Vol. 2, Book 1, Ch. 13 by Theophilus of Antioch (London: Catholic Way, 2014).

39 Cyril of Jerusalem, Trans. R.W. Church, 63-65. [language updated to reflect modern speech]

eternal life to temporal life, through Christ our Lord.[40] " (St. Ambrose of Milan)

"For after the font it remains for the 'perfecting' to take place, when, at the invocation of the priest, the Holy Spirit is bestowed, the spirit of wisdom and understanding, the spirit of counsel and strength, the spirit of knowledge and godliness, the spirit of holy fear, as it were seven virtues of the Spirit. [41]" (St. Ambrose of Milan)

"Therefore God anointed you, the Lord signed you. How? Because you were signed with the image of the cross itself unto his passion, you received a seal unto his likeness, that you may rise unto his image, and live after his pattern, who was crucified to sin and lives to God. And your old man plunged into the font was was crucified to sin, but rose again unto God. [42]" (St. Ambrose of Milan)

"No one not regenerated by the Holy Spirit of God and marked with the seal of His sanctification [Chrismation] has attained heavenly gifts, even through the perfection of a faultless life in all the rest.[43] " (St. Didymus the Blind)

"Christ and chrism are conjoined; the secret with the visible is mingled; the chrism anoints visibly, --Christ seals secretly, the lambs newborn and spiritual, the prize of His twofold victory; for He engendered it of the chrism, and He gave it birth of the water.[44] " (St. Ephrem the Syrian)

---

40 Ambrose of Milan, Trans. Rev. T. Thompson, On the Sacraments and On the Mysteries (London: S.P.C.K., 1950), 68. [language updated to reflect modern speech]

41 Ibid., 75-76

42 Ibid., 110. [language updated to reflect modern speech]

43 Didymus the Blind, De Trinitate, 2:12, quoted in Fr. Tadros Malaty, The Gift of the Holy Spirit (Cairo, Egypt: Anba Reuiss Press), 72.

44 Ephrem the Syrian, Ed. Paul A. Boer, Sr., Hymns and Homilies of St. Ephraim the Syrian,

"Christ by the hand of His servants, seals and anoints your bodies…The chrism of Christ separates the sons of the mystery from strangers: and by it they that are within are separated, and known from them that are without. [45]" (St. Ephrem the Syrian)

"The eye of faith does not observe as the physical eye observes, but faith compels the body's vision to see something that is invisible to it. [The body] sees bread and wine and oil and water, but faith compels its vision to see spiritually something that is not physically visible to it. That is, instead of bread, one shall taste the body. Instead of wine one shall drink the blood. Instead of water one shall see spiritual baptism. Instead of oil, [one shall see] the power of Christ.[46] " (St. Philoxenus of Mabbug)

"…the font of water and common oil have become the womb and the power that give birth to spiritual beings.[47] " (St. Philoxenus of Mabbug)

"But ye my brethren blessed are ye, for the fire of grace has come down, has consumed utterly your offences, and cleansed and hallowed your bodies!…The anointing of truth is this; wherein the living and all-lifegiving Blood, is sprinkled inwardly in your bodies, is mingled in your understandings, is infused through your inmost chambers. [48]" (St. Ephrem the Syrian)

(1886, reis., Edmond, OK: Veritatis Splendor, 2012), 262.

45 Ibid., 263.

46 Philoxenus of Mabbug, Trans. Robert A. Kitchen, The Discourses of Philoxenus of Mabbug (Collegeville, MN: Liturgical Press, 2013), 43.

47 Ibid., 49.

48 Ibid., 264.

"Saint Severios [Severus] said that the Myron signifies the Holy Spirit, the giver of gifts[49] " (St. Dionysius Bar Salibi)

"Just as the composition of the Myron is from oils and substances that are separate and different in essence, yet nobody says that after the composition there are many oils, but a single Myron, similarly it is not right to separate Christ, that true Myron, into two natures after the union with the flesh.[50] " (St. Dionysius Bar Salibi)

"Thus the Myron represents Christ Himself, who sanctifies and is sanctified. [51]" (St. Dionysius Bar Salibi)

"[Chrismation is] the divine and exalted mystery, more exalted and sacred than all the mysteries that the holy Church celebrates today; it is indeed the beginning of all perfections, and in it the whole priesthood is founded and perfected together. [52]" (St. Moses Bar Kepha, Bishop of Mosul)

"Without Myron the Church, the altar, the baptized, the Qurbana [Eucharist], the priests, or the deacons cannot be consecrated. [53]" (St. Moses Bar Kepha, Bishop of Mosul)

"...he who draws near to Christianity is formed by the deacons, cleansed by the hearing of the Holy Scriptures. But when he has taken hold of the way, which is faith, to come to the one true God, then he is born by baptism at the hands of the priests, and he becomes a son of God by grace, and is accounted worthy of the vision of the divine

49 Bar Salibi, Commentaries on Myron and Baptism, 20.

50 Ibid., 28.

51 Ibid., 64

52 Moses Bar Kepha, Trans. Baby Varghese, Commentary on Myron (Piscataway, NJ: Gorgias Press, 2014), 3.

53 Ibid., 79.

light…Afterwards he is signed with oil three times in the form of a cross, the priest invoking over him the Holy Trinity…That his whole body is anointed, makes known that he is entering a contest against Satan. For he also who enters the contest of a combat with men is anointed with oil, that the hands of him who contends with him may slip from him. So here also, the oil is an invincible armour against the demons…That he is sealed after he has been baptized, makes known that by the seal he receives a sweet and spiritual savour. The seal itself, moreover, is that which completes [54] the divine gifts.[55] " (St. George of the Arabs)

"The mystery of confirmation is different from that of baptism, because confirmation is a seal…by baptism we are born into the churches as children of God, whereas through confirmation we become Christ's soldiers in the face of the adversary, Satan. [56]" (St. Gregory of Tatev)

"We are baptized into Christ with water, called children of God, and united with the grace of the Holy Spirit through the oil [chrism]. [57]" (St. Gregory of Tatev)

"Ordain also a deaconess who is faithful and holy, for the ministrations towards women. For sometimes he cannot send a deacon, who is a man, to the women, on account of unbelievers. Thou shalt therefore send a woman, a deaconess, on account of the imaginations of the bad.

54 I.e., completes Baptism, grants the Spirit and His gifts, and is used to anoint the Church and Altar and the Baptismal water itself.

55 George of the Arabs, Trans. R.H. Connolly and Codrington, H.W., Two Commentaries on the Jacobite Liturgy (London: Williams and Norgate, 1913), 12-14.

56 Gregory of Tatev, Trans. Vatche Ghazarian, Homilies (Monterey, CA: Mayreni Publishing, 2018), 249.

57 Ibid., 242.

For we stand in need of a woman, a deaconess, for many necessities; and first in the baptism of women, the deacon shall anoint only their forehead with the holy oil, and after him the deaconess shall anoint them: for there is no necessity that the women should be seen by the men; but only in the laying on of hands the bishop shall anoint her head, as the priests and kings were formerly anointed, not because those which are now baptized are ordained priests, but as being Christians, or anointed, from Christ the Anointed, 'a royal priesthood, and an holy nation, the Church of God, the pillar and ground of the marriage-chamber'[58] " (Apostolic Constitutions, III.XV)

"After that, either thou, O bishop, or a presbyter that is under thee, shall in the solemn form name over them the Father, and Son, and Holy Spirit, and shall dip them in the water; and let a deacon receive the man, and a deaconess the woman, that so the conferring of this inviolable seal may take place with a becoming decency. And after that, let the bishop anoint those that are baptized with ointment. [59]" (Apostolic Constitutions, III.XVI)

"A deaconess does not bless, nor perform anything belonging to the office of presbyters or deacons, but only is to keep the doors, and to minister to the presbyters in the baptizing of women, on account of decency. [60]" (Apostolic Constitutions, VIII.XXVIII)

---

58 Schaff, ed., Vol 7, Constitutions of the Holy Apostles (London: Catholic Way, 2014).

59 Ibid.

60 Ibid.

MODERN FATHERS ON CHRISMATION

"One of the most fundamental points of the Christian life is to accept being buried with Christ in baptism to enjoy resurrection with Him. That is, to obtain new life in Christ Jesus (Rom. 6:4), and to receive the Holy Spirit through the laying on of hands for the sanctification of the soul and body together, to become a holy temple... the work of God in the believer's life, that is, to enjoy the adoption to god through baptism, and the dwelling of the Holy Spirit through the laying on of hands (or through the Myroon)[61] " (Fr. Tadros Malaty)

"[The Apostles] became the givers of the Holy Spirit by the laying on of hands and by prayer, as in appointing bishops, priests, and deacons or by the laying of hands first and then by the holy anointing as in granting the Spirit to laymen. Thus the Spirit in them started to be imparted to others in that way.

---

61 Fr. Tadros Malaty, Trans. Ferial Moawad, Hebrews (Chicago, IL: St. Mark's Coptic Orthodox Church. 1997)72-73.

Today, we administer the Sacrament of the Holy Myroun or the Holy Anointing after Baptism. In this ritual we anoint the child with Holy Myroun on numerous parts of his body, lay the hand on his head and breathe in his face, saying, 'Receive the Holy Spirit.' In administering the Sacrament to adult women, the bishop can lay his hand on their heads with prayers to receive the Holy Spirit, and anoint the apparent parts of their body [62] with the Myroun.[63] " (HH Pope Shenouda III)

"Christ has bequeathed redemption and salvation to us by shedding His blood, but it is the Holy Spirit who executes His will and makes that redemption and salvation our own right and portion. He does not make them ours through a written document[64] , but by sprinkling the heart with the blood of Christ, by washing the body in baptism and the sacramental act of unction.[65] " (Fr. Matthew the Poor)

"...as soon as we receive the Holy Spirit and are baptized and anointed and enlightened and filled with the Spirit of truth, it is as if we have declared war on the devil, and we immediately enter into the struggle with the powers of darkness and the spirit of falsehood, which holds sway

---

62 I.e., the priest or bishop only anoints the parts of a woman that are ordinarily visible and does not anoint any parts that would be inappropriate for him to touch. In the Early Church, the bishop or priest would ordinarily delegate the anointing to a Deaconess who could then anoint all of the parts of the body which are anointed on an infant when they are Chrismated.

63 HH Pope Shenouda III, The Holy Spirit and His Work in Us (London: Coptic Orthodox Publishing Association, 2015), 34.

64 I.e., this salvation is not a legal agreement. Abba Matthew is not downplaying Scripture as a means of salvation.

65 Matthew the Poor, The Communion of Love (Crestwood, NY: SVS Press, 1984), 180.

over the thinking of this world and forces it into evil and sin. [66]" (Fr. Matthew the Poor)

"As soon as a candidate is baptized with sanctified water, the officiating priest anoints him with the Oil of Catechumens, the covenantal seal of spiritual rebirth and a means of exorcism. Then the priest breathes three times on the child[67] in the form of a cross and hands him over to the godparent. [68]" (Fr. Zemene Desta)

"Christ is the Beloved with whom we are already united by Baptism and Chrismation. But that union is the beginning of a process an infinite process, of knowing the Beloved more and more deeply, becoming more and more like the Beloved.[69] " (Metropolitan Paulos Mar Gregorios)

"It is in this new humanity that Christians participate by virtue of their baptism, of their anointing with the Holy Spirit and of their participation in the body and blood of Christ. This is what really matters: the participation in this new humanity that is indivisibly and inseparably united with God. This is how I am saved- by participation in the new humanity which has overcome sin and death - not by some experience, not by my faith [alone], but by my being taken by the Grace of God into His Son's Body to be a member thereof. It is in that Body and in that new humanity that there is eternal life. [70]" (Metropolitan Paulos Mar Gregorios)

66 Ibid., 189-190.

67 This, of course, is also done with adults, though they do not necessarily need a godparent

68 Fr. Zemene Desta, Doctrinal Theology (Los Angeles, CA: Ethiopian Orthodox Tewahedo Church, 2016), 204

69 Paulos Mar Gregorios, A Human God (Kottayam, Kerala, India: Mar Gregorios Foundation, 1992), 35.

70 Ibid., 83.

"Myron Oil: is the Seal of the Holy Spirit, and it is with this oil that the child[71] is anointed after Baptism, on the body; the senses, joints and heart. All the body's organs are sanctified, and hence the body becomes a temple of the Holy Spirit. The anointing of the Myron are like a royal seal, signifying that this body is a possession of the True King and Lord Jesus Christ. The devil cannot approach it to dwell in it or possess it, as he has no dominion over it. It is possessed by the Lord Jesus and sealed by His Seal, that is, the sign of the Cross. [72]" (HG Anba Mettaous)

---

71 The Sacrament of Chrismation, of course, is given also to adult converts with the same meaning and result.

72 Anba Mettaous, Sacramental Rites in the Coptic Orthodox Church (El Sourian Monastery, Egypt: El Sourian Monastery), 25.

BIBLIOGRAPHY

Ambrose of Milan. Trans. Rev. T. Thompson. On the Sacraments and On the Mysteries. London: S.P.C.K., 1950.

Cyril of Jerusalem. Trans. R.W. Church. Lectures on the Christian Sacraments. Crestwood, NY: SVS Press, 1977.

Desta, Fr. Zemene. Doctrinal Theology. Los Angeles, CA: Ethiopian Orthodox Tewahedo Church, 2016.

Didymus the Blind. De Trinitate. 2:12. Quoted in Fr. Tadros Malaty. The Gift of the Holy Spirit. Cairo, Egypt: Anba Reuiss Press. Page 72.

Ephrem the Syrian. Ed. Paul A. Boer, Sr. Hymns and Homilies of St. Ephraim the Syrian. Edmond, OK: Veritatis Splendor, 2012. A Select Library of the Nicene and Post-Nicene Fathers of the Christian Church, Vol. 13. Ed. Philip Schaff. Buffalo, NY: The Christian Literature Co. 1886.

Gregory of Tatev. Trans. Vatche Ghazarian. Homilies. Monterey, CA: Mayreni Publishing, 2018.

Malaty, Fr. Tadros. Trans. Ferial Moawad. Hebrews. Chicago, IL: St. Mark's Coptic Orthodox Church. 1997.

Matthew the Poor. The Communion of Love. Crestwood, NY: SVS Press. 1984.

Mettaous, Anba. Sacramental Rites in the Coptic Orthodox Church. El Sourian Monastery, Egypt: El Sourian Monastery.

Moses Bar Kepha. Trans. Baby Varghese. Commentary on Myron. Piscataway, NJ: Gorgias Press, 2014.

Ormanian, Archbishop Malachia. The Church of Armenia. Burbank, CA: WDACNA, 2007.

Papazian, Michael. The Doctor of Mercy. Collegeville, MN:Liturgical Press Academic, 2019.

Philoxenus of Mabbug. Trans. Robert A. Kitchen. The Discourses of Philoxenus of Mabbug. Collegeville, MN: Liturgical Press, 2013.

Philip Schaff, ed. The Complete Ante-Nicene & Nicene and Post-Nicene Church Fathers Collection. London: Catholic Way, 2014.

Serapion of Thmuis. Trans. Dr. G. Wobbermin. Bishop Sarapion's Prayer Book. London: SPCK, 1899.

Shenouda III, HH Pope. The Holy Spirit and His Work in Us. London: Coptic Orthodox Publishing Association, 2015.